Child Custody, Visitation *and* Child Support *in New York*

Answers and Advice to the Most Common Family Law Questions

NY | FLG

Written by The New York Family Law Group

Co-Authored by

Martin Mohr and Ethan Steward

New York Family Law Group
184 East 161st Street
Bronx, NY 10451
718-293-1542
www.NewYorkFamilyLawGroup.com

Ordering Information:

Quantity sales. Special discounts are available on quantity purchases by corporations, associations, and others. For details, contact the publisher at the address above.

Orders by U.S. trade bookstores and wholesalers. Please contact Martin Mohr: Tel: (718) 293-1542 or e-mail help@newyorkfamilylawgroup.com

Printed in the United States of America

Published in 2021

PREFACE

Bringing a child into the world is an enormous responsibility. There is no instruction manual providing directions on how to raise them. No matter how hard you search there is no perfect way to do it. One size does not fit all, and results will vary. No guide to get you to the easy joy filled days or through the difficult curve balls that will be throw your way. When difficult times approach, some times without warning, that will affect you and your family the thought of navigating a legal issue in court is something you must do with trusted legal resources. A team of professionals that has been there before and will get you where you want to be. Some of our collective legal experiences are within this book to assist you in that journey.

DEDICATION

This book is dedicated to every parent who wants the best for their children.

Disclaimer

This book is ***not*** intended to provide legal advice or to interfere with any established legal relationship you may have with an attorney. The information in this book does not form any attorney client relationship with the reader. Rather, our intention is to provide guidance and suggestions on the legal process of custody, separation, and divorce.

New York Family Law Group
184 East 161st Street
Bronx, NY 10451
(718) 293-1542
www.newyorkfamilylawgroup.com

TESTIMONIALS

"I decided to meet Mr. Mohr after even having a detailed conversation on the phone with him; with this issue that I am being dealt with. He made me feel so secured and promised me not to worry, He talks to you like he knows you already , told me exactly the three options on what we can do going forward, and put me at ease, it was the first time since this ongoing issue that I went home feeling less stressed out. even made extra time to explain things to my daughter. I highly recommend Mr. Mohr to anyone and everyone! Btw it was the first and only lawyer I met for this, no need to go anywhere else!!!!"

– Maggie C.

****

"Mr. Mohr is a very knowledgeable and reasonable attorney who was very helpful in the petition I filed for my visitation order enforcement. He is efficient and gives great advice so that you get the outcome you are looking and you are not making multiple trips to court. He's a good listener and has reasonable rates."

– Nityanan

****

"I can't thank Mr. Mohr enough for representing me during my custody and child support case. He was very knowledgeable and helpful to me during a very stressful case. I will highly recommend him to anyone in need of legal advice and representation!"

– Nandrani

****

"He is a great lawyer, he was fast and efficient and made sure that my concerns were voiced and heard fairly and accurately. He is very in tuned with his clients and I would recommend him to anyone. Thanks Again."

– Sylvia

****

"I had a wonderful experience working with Mr. Mohr and his team, they are so helpful, respectful and professional. I really recommend them!"

– Meybol B.

****

"Exceptional lawyer but even more so an all around good man! Thanks, Mr. Mohr, for everything I appreciate you!"

– Ashley N.

****

TABLE OF CONTENTS

INTRODUCTION

If you're reading this book, then you are likely trying to figure out whether you need to buckle up for a bumpy post-relationship breakup, or are headed towards an amicable, civil uncoupling with your soon-to-be ex. You may be wondering whether you will be able to maintain your relationship with your children, and even your own sanity. There may be a number of other questions running through your mind, like: Am I financially prepared for the upcoming lifestyle and parenting schedule adjustments? Do I need to talk to an attorney? Will I have to go to court, and if so, where? What's the next most important step I need to take?

The process of trying to determine the right way to move forward and the best solution for your family can be difficult and stressful. During such times, many people turn to the internet for answers, just like they do when shopping for a new car, shoes, or a good movie to watch. When it comes to deciding on a new item to purchase, most people begin by reading reviews, and searching for the right attorney to handle an impending divorce and custody matter should be no different—with the exception that there is a whole lot more weighing on the decisions you make.

This book is designed to help you solve the problems that arise when a relationship is coming to an end. There are some surefire ways to spend years embroiled in a court battle fighting with your ex, just as there are ways to make smart decisions that are in your children's best interests, and that will encourage a healthful co-parenting relationship with your ex. Ultimately, the goal is for you to transition as smoothly as possible into the next chapter of your life, so that you can begin to make new memories and leave the bad ones behind.

CHAPTER 1

HOW DO I START? THE BASICS OF YOUR FAMILY MATTER IN NEW YORK STATE

The first step in handling a family matter is to determine whether you will need court intervention. Do you want a judge—an absolute stranger—to be responsible for making decisions that will forever impact your life and the lives of your children? This is a question that you must consider, first and foremost. Most people who are being honest with themselves will answer this question with an affirmative and bold

"NO." Unfortunately, depending on the circumstances of your case, traditional litigation could become necessary, regardless of your answer.

The Supreme Court vs. Family Court

If you decide that you need the assistance of the Court system, the second step is to determine whether your matter will be heard by the Family Court or the Supreme Court of New York State; the answer may be dictated by the nature of your relationship with the parent of your children.

If you are legally married to the parent of your children, then the Supreme Court will have exclusive decision-making authority in terms of whether you can get a divorce. However, the decision to grant a divorce in the Supreme Court does not usually require a trial, because New York follows a no-fault-based system. This means that you no longer need to have grounds for divorce, and one party cannot prevent the divorce from happening. For instance, the reason for the divorce could simply be that you and your spouse no longer get along. This no-fault-based system makes the divorce process easier.

In theory, both the Supreme Court and the Family Court have jurisdiction at any point after a divorce has been entered in the Supreme Court. An exception that the Supreme Court may retain exclusive jurisdiction, and can only be heard in Supreme Court is possible but very unlikely to occur. However, both courts will have jurisdiction over any custody, visitation, or child support issue.

When divorce cases are decided, the courts will often say that future issues can be litigated in a court of competent jurisdiction. A competent jurisdiction would be either the Supreme Court or Family Court. There is one NYC local rule, however, which specifies that if a divorce from the Supreme Court took place within the last 18 months, then the Family Court would have to refer the case back to the Supreme Court.

There are several reasons for this rule, the main one being that there is a presumption that the Supreme Court addressed and dealt with all of the issues. If parties went back and forth between Supreme Court and Family Court, individuals would be asking a new judge in Family Court to change the decisions that were recently just decided by the Supreme Court.

If a period of 18 months has passed and you want to modify a child support decision, going to Family Court might be the preferred route. A decision to modify an order, will be quicker and less costly to obtain in family court. You can still get a modification from the Supreme Court where the case was decided, but it will be more formal and costly. By contrast, there are no filing fees in Family Court.

The primary focus in the Supreme Court is reaching an agreement about custody and visitation issues. If you and the other party cannot reach an agreement, the first step is to have a conference with the judge's court attorney. It can be helpful to get an impression from the judge on their view of the decisions that need to be made by the court; this skill is developed by attorneys over many appearances before a judge, and may help you move forward without fruitless reward for your hard-earned money and valuable time.

In the Supreme Court, absent a trial, much of the negotiation regarding custody and visitation will initially take place between the attorneys. In general, there is more collaboration between the attorneys and litigants prior to seeing a judge in the supreme court. That said, both courts encourage parties—regardless of whether they are married—to find resolution on their own, without the need for trial.

Turning to Family Court, it is possible that the Family Court will resolve some issues, which can also be incorporated into a divorce agreement in Supreme Court. In other words, instead of re-litigating those issues, they could simply be incorporated into the judge's divorce decision.

The decisions that are made in Family Court are determined by laws in the New York Family Court Act. The family court hears and makes determinations on custody and visitation cases, orders of protection cases, guardianship cases, child protective matters, child support matters, and juvenile delinquency cases.

If you are not legally married to the parent of your children, then you will be dealing with the legal issues of custody, visitation, and child support in Family Court. All cases in Family Court are "special proceedings" and can be commenced quickly and without the costs required in Supreme Court.

Procedural Differences

Procedurally, the Supreme Court and Family Court of New York State are somewhat similar. The first step is to draft legal documents and serve them to the other party (these documents are generally handed to the other parent in person). At that point, the other parent will be made aware that you plan to initiate litigation against them. For example, you could file a petition in Family Court seeking custody of your children, or you may file a complaint in the Supreme Court for a divorce to address the legal issues.

In both the Supreme Court and Family Court, a trial date or several dates will be selected for a dispute that cannot be resolved. At trial, the first step is for the parties to assemble and get sworn in. If you filed your case first, then the trial will begin with you, regardless of whether it's taking place in the Supreme Court or Family Court.

Depending on the purpose of the court appearance, several common items can be a part of the agenda. For example, for a visitation matter, reports ordered by the court about the progress of supervised visitation, Administration for Children's Services ("ACS") investigations, and forensic reports may be provided and then discussed by the parties; for a custody matter, you will need to demonstrate why you would be the more fit parent since the law presumes that both parents are considered fit.

In-Court vs. Virtual Appearances

In March of 2020, the coronavirus pandemic caused a lot of changes to the way society goes about its business, and the court system is no different. Almost all cases in the New York Statewide court system were being heard virtually including New York City. Each party is given a separate link and a phone number to call. You should be prepared with that information as soon as possible and check your connections. You should also be in a place where it is quiet and distraction-free, which means ensuring that your children and anyone else in the house doesn't interrupt the court proceeding. There is no recording, rebroadcasting, or screenshots allowed.

As the grip of the Pandemic lossens court appearances will begin to be in person. While virtual court appearances will not continue forever, the court is likely to use some type of virtual court procedures going forward. In part, this is because litigants and jurists have benefitted from virtual procedures. Sitting in your own home waiting for a court appearance usually beats sitting in a courthouse for hours on end. It should be noted that appearing virtually is no different than being there in person, meaning the same rules of dress and behavior apply.

It is important to understand what to expect for in-court appearances. For many, going to court is a strange and uncomfortable experience, especially if it is the first time being involved in a legal matter. And when that legal matter is about your children or former partner, rather than a simple traffic ticket or civil case, the stakes are even higher, as are the level of emotions.

If you are set to appear in person, then you will need to arrive to the courthouse early, since you won't know whether there will be a long line. You will be expected to remove everything from your pockets before passing through a metal detector, much like you would at the airport. Once you have passed the metal detector, you will find the floor where your case will be heard, and sit in a waiting room until your case is called. In some ways, it is like waiting at a doctor's office.

Once you and the other party are called and brought into the courtroom, the court proceeding will occur. Each attorney will make their arguments, and the decision will be made by the judge. The judges' ruling will be written on paper by the court clerk and signed by the judge and distributed to you and the other party. Read your order before you leave the courthouse. Sometimes errors occur and it is easier to fix when you are still in court.

Following the court order, you will leave the courtroom, and should be prepared for the unexpected. For instance, did your soon-to-be ex bring their parents and friends—or even worse—their new significant other? Did someone bring the child whom you've not seen in months? Is your phone about to die because you didn't expect to be in the courthouse all day? Are you getting hungry because you figured there would at least be vending machines? It is just as important to be prepared for what you do not expect as it is to be prepared for what you do expect when making an in-court appearance.

CHAPTER 2

WHAT SHOULD I EXPECT? THE DETERMINATION OF PHYSICAL AND LEGAL CUSTODY IN NEW YORK STATE

There are two types of custody in New York. The first is legal custody, which refers to which parent will make major legal decisions for the children. Major decisions generally include medical, schooling, and religious decisions. Regular day-to-day decisions are usually left to the parent who is providing care for the child at the time. For example, a trip to the doctor to treat an allergy, regular cold, or infection is ***not*** considered a major decision.

In about 95 percent of cases, the major decisions about religion have been addressed, leaving decisions about medical and school outstanding. Generally, extracurricular activities are excluded as a major decision but need to be considered when scheduling parenting time. When planning extracurricular activities, it is a good idea to clear that activity with the other parent so that it does not interfere with the other parent's parenting schedule.

Physical custody is the second type of custody in New York. Physical Custody refers to the parent with whom the child lives most of the time (i.e., the custodial parent). The non-custodial parent is referred to as the visiting parent. There is no one-size-fits-all for a visiting parent. A parenting plan needs to be custom-tailored to each family, and guidance from an attorney in this area is extremely valuable.

Importantly, when parties are legally married, the law presumes that the parties have joint legal custody; this is usually a significant delineation when going to the Supreme Court, because the judge is most likely to think that the parties should share major decision-making choices about their lives and the lives of their children.

In an uncontested divorce, the court can leave the decision of custody matters up to the parents. An uncontested divorce is much simpler than a contested divorce, because it usually involves parties who are on the same page about major issues like custody, visitation, parenting time, and child support. Their agreement can be drafted into a document that will be signed by both parties, and then submitted to the court with various other documents for the judge to approve. While sample uncontested divorce forms can be obtained from the court's website, they must be completed accurately. Failure to do this could result in the court returning the forms, requesting changes, which will delay the divorce process and cost valuable time and money.

When parties have children together but are unmarried, the resolution might be a bit more difficult since there is no presumption of joint legal custody. These situations carry an extra layer of complication because parents have beliefs about visitation, and sole versus joint legal custody.

Factors Considered by the Court

If you and the other parent are unable or unwilling to create a solution for the custody dispute, then the only remaining option will be to force the courts to make the decision for you and your family. In determining which parent should be the physical and legal custodian of a child, the courts consider many factors. It's important to keep in mind that most of the decisions are not about whether a parent is able to care for the many needs of the child, but which parent can do this better than the other. This comparison by each parent as to who does what better will not result in the parties getting along with one another.

While the following list of considerations is not exhaustive, it covers the most common ones:

- Which parent is better able to support the children financially, by securing an income sufficient to support the children?
- Which parent is better able to support the children emotionally?
- Which parent is better able to provide a sufficient amount of time to activities and events for the children?
- Where would each parent enroll their children in school, and would it be a private or public school?
- Which parent's educational background will better support the children's educational needs?
- Where would the children be living?
- What type of housing will each parent's living arrangement provide for the children?
- Will one or the other parent's living arrangement mean that the children will have relatives (e.g., siblings and stepsiblings) or extended family living with them or nearby?

- What are the children's stated or unstated wishes, or what is the recommendation of their attorney?
- What does each parent have to say to the judge?
- Are there any court orders or requirements that each parent must follow?
- Has there been domestic unrest or violence in the home?
- Which parent is better able to promote or willing to foster a relationship with the non-custodial parent?
- Which parent is going to encourage collaboration or co-parenting with the other parent?
- Does one parent disparage the other parent or talk badly about the other parent's family members?
- Does one parent miss or cancel visits with the children?
- Has one parent already demonstrated that they are unable to follow court orders?

All of the above-mentioned factors can be used to determine physical and legal custody if a trial needs to proceed in family court. These factors may be used in the supreme court to help mold a resolution, either with or without a trial.

The Child's Voice

One of the most common questions asked by a parent about the legal process is whether their child can speak in court and tell the judge whether they would prefer to live with one parent over the other. While this is usually good-intentioned, imagine actually asking your child to testify before a room full of strangers, and essentially choose one parent over the other; this, in all likelihood, would not be in the best interests of the child.

A child doesn't directly speak or make decisions with the judge during the proceeding. However, children who can communicate meaningfully with other adults will be assigned an attorney at the very beginning of the case. This attorney is referred to as an attorney for the child (AFC).

Without directly asking the child which parent they would prefer to live with, the AFC is responsible for ascertaining the child's position on custody and visitation matters through conversations with the child. Having gained specialized knowledge through years of training, the AFC is a professional who is equipped with the ability to ask the child the right questions in the right way to determine the answer to this question: "Who do you want to live with?"

The AFC will know which questions will lead the child to explain what types of activities they participate in with each parent, what each parent contributes to their life, and how much they enjoy their relationship with each parent. The information acquired from asking the right questions will enable the AFC to form an opinion about whether the child would prefer to live with one or the other parent.

In addition to being represented by an attorney at court conferences and trial, the Court may decide to conduct an in-camera interview with the child. An in-camera interview takes place privately with the judge and the AFC. Outside your presence, your child will meet the judge in their office or courtroom. The judge may ask similar questions that were asked by the AFC in order to form an opinion about your child's position on who they would prefer to live with. The answer to the questions may or may not be consistent with the questions that were already asked by the AFC. The inclusion of the camera is to help the judge better understand the child's position with respect to physical and legal custody.

The age of the child is very important; the older the child, the more likely it is that the judge will find their position compelling, and use it to determine the outcome of some major decisions.

A note about talking to you children about your case: As tempting as it may be, do ***NOT*** talk to your children about your case, directly or indirectly. Even at a very young age, children have the ability to recognize discord in your relationship. Asking them to tell their attorney or the judge something specific will backfire more often than not, and is easily detected by anyone who has been trained to talk to and understand children.

What is a Forensic Exam?

Depending on the complexity of the case and the legal issues that are presented, a court may order you and the other party to submit to a forensic evaluation with a licensed doctor or therapist. The doctor or therapist will act as an independent third party and ask questions of you, the other party, and the children.

During the evaluations, it is not uncommon for each parent's interaction with their children to be observed. The doctor or therapist will watch the interaction between the parent and child, as well as conduct collateral interviews with the other members of the family and other people who interact with the children, such as school teachers or babysitters. The report that is generated from these observations and interviews is confidential, so you will not have access to a copy of it, nor will the other parent. However, you may be allowed to review the report in the presence of your attorney.

The report is a recommendation to the court, and alongside the in-camera interview, will provide the judge with more information than they had previously. While neither the report nor the interview is dispositive of the final outcome, the judge will certainly consider it in their decision-making process. For instance, if a child says, "I want to live with my mommy," it doesn't mean that the judge will determine, on that fact alone, that the child will live with the mother.

Similarly, any recommendations made by the forensic examiner (namely, what each parent should do in order to establish and/or maintain a healthy parent-child relationship), may not impact the judge's decision regarding custody, visitation, or parenting time. Recommendations for promoting the parent-child relationship may include individual, family, or joint therapy between parent and child, participation in an alcohol or drug treatment program, or parenting classes to address potential deficiencies.

It's important to understand that the forensic exam interviews can be not only time-consuming, but intrusive and even a bit embarrassing, because you will be asked to provide information that you would not normally share with a stranger.

The report will be forwarded to the court and the attorneys, but it won't automatically become part of the trial. Instead, each attorney can review the report with their client, and the attorneys can possibly help facilitate a resolution between the parents. The downside to ordering these reports is that they are lengthy and can be expensive. The evaluation can take two to four months to complete, and it's not uncommon for the evaluation itself to take more than four months.

In combination, the evidence presented at trial, the forensic evaluation, the judge's interview with the child, and ultimately the judge's determination will leave you with a decision that you or the other parent may not like. Now is a good time to remind you of a key take away from chapter one, you might not want a stranger to decide how you're going to live the rest of your life.

The Determination of Sole Physical And Legal Custody

In order for the courts to grant sole physical and legal custody to one parent, the factors the court considers would have to overwhelmingly lean in one parent's direction. There are several factors discussed above that Court's consider when making such a determination. One such factor is domestic violence. A court may grant sole custody to one parent if there is a history of domestic violence or active orders of protection precluding one parent from talking to the other, or if one parent is unable to co-parent with the other parent; in either case, making joint decisions would be problematic. A court can determine that sole legal decision-making would be in the children's best interest if the parties cannot work out issues effectively.

It's an extreme measure for the court to grant sole physical and legal custody to one parent and exclude the non-custodial parent from having any visitation, but it can happen. All of the factors that were discussed earlier will help a court make the determination that one parent is more fit to be the physical or legal custodian of the child.

If the court determines that one parent should be granted sole physical and legal custody of the children, then the other parent will be unable to make any major decisions regarding medical care, dental care, education, and religion. However, it can be ordered or agreed that the non-custodial parent should have independent access to speak with their children's doctors or contact the children's teachers in order to determine how their child is doing.

One parent being granted physical or legal custody will not preclude someone from returning to court to address something which they believe is not in the best interests of the children. For example, if the physical and legal custodian of the children decides to send the children away to a boarding school, it could negatively impact the non-custodial parent and/or children by eliminating the ability to exercise a parenting schedule.

CHAPTER 3

CUSTODY, VISITATION, AND CHILD SUPPORT

Child Support and Custody are Completely Separate

There is a lot of misunderstanding about the relationship between custody and visitation and child support and the impact one has on the other. Parents might believe not paying child support should mean that the other parent is not entitled to visitation. Conversely, simply paying child support does not automatically entitle a parent to visit with their child. Believing that one is contingent on the other happening causes a tremendous amount of friction between parties, and can detrimentally impact the child

In New York, custody and visitation is separate and apart from child support. They are mutually exclusive.

In fact two completely different jurists make decisions on those legal issues.

A judge or referee hears the application for custody and visitation, while a support magistrate decides child support applications, all of which occur in Family Court.

If you are not receiving child support payments, then you can seek a court order enforcing payment of child support. Additionally, if the parent is willfully failing to make ordered child support payments, then they could be sentenced to jail. Conversely, if you deny visitation to the other parent because they are not paying child support, then you could potentially face drastic consequences—including a court order which removes custody of the children from you, and grants it to the other parent.

Exchanging Children Between Parents with Joint Physical Custody or Visitation

Most court orders include a specific location for pick-ups and drop-offs of the children. A court can order that pick-ups and drop-offs occur at a local precinct, curbside at one parent's home, a community-based location, or a public place.

In general, designated pick-up and drop-off locations are ordered by the court when there is a history of violence or conflict between the parents. If one party has an order of protection against the other, then the pick-up and drop-off location will likely be at a precinct.

Parties should strongly consider the best place for exchanges. Many people enjoy a great level of comfort by having exchanges occur at a police precinct. It may be convenient to the adult and give some security to the parent who is picking up or dropping off the child. However, it is recommended that parents take a step back and consider things from the perspective of a young child, which might encourage them to realize that for a young child, being exposed to a police precinct might not necessarily be the best option. Instead, it may better to have a third party do the pick-ups and drop-offs at another place. There are many creative ways to arrange pick-ups and drop-offs that are in the children's best interest.

Supervised Visitation

Some circumstances or allegations can lead a court to order supervised visitation, which is an issue that arises frequently in custody cases. It's not uncommon for one parent to want the other parent to have supervised visitation with the children, meaning that someone else would need to observe and evaluate the visits between the children and the parent.

Depending on the circumstances, the court may determine that supervised visitation is appropriate, either on a temporary or long-term basis. For example, allegations of substance abuse, corporal punishment, and extended absence by one parent are legitimate reasons a court may order supervised visitation. If the children do not want to see one parent, then therapeutic visitation may be ordered.

The agency that conducts the supervised visitation usually submits a court report for review by the court, which will be distributed to the parties. Once distributed to the parties, the parties' attorneys can review it with their clients. At that point, the court may or may not choose to continue supervised visitation. However, courts do not have the ability to monitor supervised visitation forever. It is not uncommon for a case to start with supervised visitation and progress to unsupervised day or overnight visitation. It is important to note that the parties may be responsible for paying for supervised visitation.

CHAPTER 4

CAN MY EX AND I WORK TOGETHER? EFFECTIVE AND POSITIVE CO-PARENTING

Co-parenting between parents is extremely important for children; it's important for them to understand that their parents are parenting them similarly, even though they're living in separate places. No one doubts that each parent has a strong bond, cares for, and loves their child. Co-parenting is a skill that parents learn and a behavior that children learn from, and there are many resources that show effective ways to co-parent. Parents do not have to love each other anymore, but they certainly must be able to work together for the benefit of their children.

The relationship between you and the other parent may be over to the extent that you're no longer cohabitating and sharing daily activities with one another, but you will still share life events for many years to come, especially if your children are young. Your children will want to see both of their parents at important events and activities, like school graduations and weddings and other life cycle events. That is when you will be grateful that you have managed to effectively co-parent for the benefit of your children. You'll want to show your children by example that, just because their parents are no longer living together, it doesn't mean they can't get along and be civil towards each other.

A child certainly learns both positive and negative behaviors that are exhibited by their parents, and this can be a major factor when a court decides which parent should be granted custody of the children. If you promote a healthy relationship with the other parent, this behavior will likely be modeled by them. For example, if your seven-year-old son observes that you show negative behaviors toward the other parent, then your son may start to think that that is how he should be treated or treat others in his future relationships.

As a parent you should take steps to demonstrate healthy behavior is to help your child pick out a Mother's Day or Father's Day card for the other parent. This behavior demonstrates to your child conventional behavior they have previously been accustomed to can be reshaped to acknowledge those conventional occasions in a different way. In other words, even though your relationship with your ex has changed and purchasing a Mother's Day card is something that you would do, it demonstrates to you child how to respect and honor their mother. This also is a way to promote healthy co-parenting between parents.

Another way to foster healthy co-parenting would be to have a discussion with your children about the rules and expected behaviors that apply regardless of whether they are staying in your home or the other parent's home. For instance, bedtime routines should be similar at both parents' houses. This doesn't mean that the bedtime needs to be the exact same in each home, but if there is a major disparity, there could be unintended consequences when it's time for school the next day. If the other parent has an established routine that you interrupt every time you see the children, then expect complaints.

If there are methods of discipline in one home, they should be carried over into the other home. For example, if your daughter is doing poorly in school because she is distracted by her cell phone, then you and the other parent should agree that an appropriate punishment might be to take away her cell phone. Sending different messages depending on whose household the child is in only invites discord; if the other parent has punished your child for not doing their homework, then you should enforce that same punishment when your child is staying with you.

It is important that you and the other parent communicate effectively about the medical needs of your children. For example, if your child is taking medication, whether on a temporary or long-term basis, both you and the other parent need to ensure that you have the medication with you when taking care of the child, and that you know how frequently the child should be taking the medication.

Another co-parenting best practice is to decide how the child will travel between homes. Rather than children being responsible for taking their belongings to and from each home, consider having their own clothes at each home. If your child gets picked up from school on a Friday afternoon, having to pack clothes and lug them over to the other parent's house for the weekend might not be comfortable or easy. This is a solution that may work for everyone including your child.

Finally, and probably the most important rule about co-parenting. You should not talk to a child about an ongoing or completed court case! Your child will have their own attorney with whom to discuss the proceedings. You should not disparage other family members or the other parent in front of your child. Even for a young child, it is easy for them to sense when their parents are fighting, and you don't want your children to think that combative behavior is appropriate.

The Tough Decisions and Tie-Breakers

Parents commonly make joint decisions about their children, such as what medical treatment they will receive or where they will go to school. Reaching an agreement isn't always an easy task. So, what options are available to you if you are unable to reach an agreement with the other parent?

One option is to have an agreement which dictates that if an agreement cannot be reached, the custodial parent should have the final say (this is often referred to as having the authority to make the tie-breaker decisions).

A less common way to prevent such disagreements is for each parent to be responsible for one or more major decisions. Referred to as a sphere of influence, under this agreement you might be responsible for making final decisions about medical care, and the other parent might be responsible for making final decisions about education.

In some cases, mediation with a formal license mediator will be required before you and the other parent can return to court over a disagreement.

Yet another way to avoid ending up back in court is to agree in advance that a third party will help resolve any major decisions that can't otherwise be decided. For example, you and the other parent could decide that if an agreement cannot be reached regarding a medical issue in the future, the child's pediatrician will be allowed to explain to both parents the reasons for the diagnosis and recommended treatment, and make the decision.

Similarly, you and the other parent could decide that if an agreement cannot be reached regarding an educational issue in the future, the child's teacher or guidance counselor can explain to both parents why a particular educational need is recommended.

The hope is that after reading this, you and every other parent out there will conclude that making every possible effort to reach an agreement on a particular decision is the ideal way to co-parent.

A few words of caution: For many people, part of this transition will involve finding a new partner. However, it is usually best to avoid entering a new relationship while in the middle of a divorce or custody case; it might not only complicate matters, but also create acrimony between you and your ex, which is the last thing you need.

To help a new relationship succeed, certain steps may need to be taken prior to allowing the new significant other to enter the lives of your children. You should keep in mind that meeting a new significant other who doesn't end up sticking around for long can be very confusing for children. For this reason, the wisest decision may be to refrain from introducing a new partner into the day-to-day life of your children until the divorce and custody issue is resolved, and you are confident that your new relationship will be long-lasting.

CHAPTER 5

SHOULD I DO IT MYSELF? PRO SE LITIGANTS VS. HIRING AN ATTORNEY TO REPRESENT YOU

Attempting to navigate the court system on your own, or as a pro se litigant, has many potential pitfalls that can cost you time, money, and energy you can't afford. One of the biggest pitfalls is overlooking certain legal issues and requirements, like specific filing deadlines which must be met.

Often, the terminology used in court is confusing or has special meaning. Without a legal background this can be very difficult to understand. Don't expect help from the judge or the other parent's attorney; if you're representing yourself in court as a pro se litigant, the court is going to expect you to know the court procedure, rules of evidence, when to make objections how to examine and cross examine a witness.

No matter how confident you are in your grasp of the elements of a family law case, you likely have a weak spot somewhere, and the last place you want that weak spot exposed is in the middle of a trial, with major life decisions on the line. It's like being on a TV game show: The answers to the questions seem easy, but when you're participating in the game, for some reason, things become much more difficult. It might not even be that you don't know the information, but that there's just a lot more unanticipated pressure.

Simply, parents that represent themselves in family court or the Supreme court will do more damage than they realize and often the mistakes can't be fixed. Even with a matter as simple as an uncontested divorce application, it is exceedingly easy to make one error or inaccuracy that slows the entire process and costs you time and money. Having a seasoned attorney represent you in court or handle the paperwork is invaluable.

It is very important to recognize that the role of an attorney is to provide information based on their experienced professional opinion. In much the same way that you would go to a doctor to ask about a medical prognosis or treatment for an injury, you should go to an attorney to discuss your family law matter, ask for recommendations regarding next steps, and ensure that you aren't overlooking anything that could harm your case.

The benefits of having an attorney far outweigh the risks of representing yourself. The right attorney will have been battle-tested in court and through a lifetime of experience in dealing with and preventing major issues. They will feel at home in the courtroom, they'll be prepared for things you didn't even think possible, they'll know the rules and procedures, and they will even be familiar with the judges.

This experience will have a significant impact on the way the case travels through the court system, and will ensure that you do not fall victim to the many pitfalls encountered by those who choose to represent themselves.

The New York Family Law Group

NY | FLG

Focusing on What Matters to You

At the New York Family Law Group, we offer our clients a team centric approach to solving your legal matter. Seasoned staff and paralegals are there to support our attorneys with more than three decades' worth of experience in navigating the difficult and often emotional issues inherent in family law. More importantly, we can relate to our clients on a personal level, because we have been where they are, and we have endured the same feelings and struggles. We want to help people resolve their family law matters in the simplest, most efficient, and most compassionate way possible in order to enable them to confidently move forward to the next chapter of their lives.

INDEX

NOTES

Made in the USA
Monee, IL
05 November 2026

67378079R00038